the little
Adobo
book

Gene Gonzalez

Anvil

The Little Àdobo Book
Gene Gonzalez

Copyright @ GENE GONZALEZ, 1999

Published and exclusively distributed by
ANVIL PUBLISHING, INC.
8007-B Pioneer St., Bgy. Kapitolyo, Pasig City 1603 Philippines
Tels.: 6373621, 6375141 (sales & marketing)
Fax: 6376084
Email: anvilsales@eudoramail.com

Front cover photo by Edith Morales
Back cover photo by Wig Tysmans
Cover photo concept by Mildred Cid
Cover design by Gerry Baclagon
Interior design by Dencel L. Aquino & Ani V. Habúlan
Food Styling by Eugene Raymundo
Illustrations by Moises Nicolas

First printing, 1999
Fourth printing, 2004

ISBN 971-27-0817-9

Printed in the Philippines
by The House Printers, Inc.

adobo

I thought about a series of little books on Philippine cuisine and beverages as an easy, fast guide for today's cosmopolitan kitchens and busy bodies.

This first book in a series shows the ease of method and preparations for Philippine *adobo*, a simple dish that transcends gastronomic incompatibilities between Philippine regions and ethnic groups, each having their own versions of this cooking method plus its appeal to foreign visitors who find these dishes representative of true tropical cuisine.

Adobo to a Filipino is about as basic as one can get. It is a dish that can be served for breakfast, lunch or dinner or even for a round of friendly drinking. When one is unsure about the ingredient to be cooked, one simply makes an adobo. The miracle of flavors happens when a few pieces of chopped garlic infuses with spritzes of vinegar and blends with the other ingredients producing a truly appetizing yet simple and economical dish.

So here's the little Adobo book, a book that transgresses all seasons and culinary moods.

introduction

Before the coming of the Spaniards, the early Philippine inhabitants had used this cooking method of braising in vinegar and spices to increase the longevity of their food in a tropical climate when there was no refrigeration.

In the old days, when freezers were unheard of, the cooks had to rely on the *sangkutsa* method of pre-cooking in bulk. This consisted of slicing the meat into big chunks and pre-cooking them. These were half fried in plenty of lard and sautéed in a lot of garlic, onions and salt. A little *sukang Iloko* (called *vinagre* in Bulacan) was poured in."

What turned out to be an ancestral cooking method is now being referred to as the Philippine national dish because of its appeal even to foreign tastes. Adobo is part of every Filipino table and is practical because

---

Philippine Food and Life, Gilda Cordero-Fernando, Anvil Publishing, Pasig, Metro Manila, 1992, p. 28.

v

of the ease of preparation and simplicity of ingredients.

Regional variations of the dish feature plentiful items found in the provinces where some of the recipes in this book are found. Taste can vary greatly with the addition of coco cream or lemongrass or a sauté in *achuete* (annatto)-infused oil or turmeric. Vinegar such as palm, cane, pineapple, *basi* (sugarcane wine) give different dimensions as in *patis* or fermented fish sauce that could use anchovies, shrimps or other types of seafood. Cross-cultural mixes have given adobo other nuances such as the use of ngo-hiong (five-spice powder), *toyo* (soy sauce), rice wine and even Worcestershire sauce.

This book would have not been possible if not for the encouragement of three talented apprentices: Jennifer Tiano, Carla Ledesma, and Christine Paredes who pushed and prodded me to finally start writing and testing a small piece of yellowing paper they found posted on my refrigerator door the past two years. This was the outline of the little Adobo book and little did my students realize the start of their miniature nightmares when I had them test and improve the recipes I had compiled.

Special thanks also to Gino's Fine Dining, Chef Rizalina Chua and DJ Deloso, my assistant, Meg Soriano and Celia Padilla, manager of Lasap: Pagkaing Pilipino for their great cooperation and support.

And of course, to our Lord above who has given us many pleasures of the kitchen and table so that we may appreciate and enjoy the fruits of His creation.

contents

x

basic Philippine adobo

INGREDIENTS

700 gms. pork (preferably
 with fat from the belly
 or back portion)
3 tbsps. vinegar
1/4 tsp. cracked peppercorns
8 large cloves of garlic or
 2 small fresh native garlic
1/2 tsp. salt
2 tbsps. patis
2 tbsp. oil

procedure

Sauté garlic in oil until golden brown. Add pork and stir-fry until brown. Add vinegar and simmer. Don't stir until vinegar boils and releases its acidic odor. Add pepper, patis and continue simmering until pork is tender.

the chef says:

Variations to a basic adobo recipe vary from family to family such as the addition of bay leaf or soy sauce to the basic dish. Others put fresh green peppercorns or the actual peppercorn leaves.

1

adobong crispy pata
crispy pork shoulder adobo

INGREDIENTS
1 kg. pork shoulder
1 tsp. curry powder
1/2 tsp. salt and 1/2 tsp. pepper
1 pc. onion, chopped
2 pcs. laurel leaves
50 gms. pork, chopped
4 tbsps. vinegar
2 tbsps. soy sauce
1 laurel leaf
4 cloves garlic, minced
MSG to taste
a pinch of ground pepper
1/2 cup pork broth

procedure

Marinate the pork shoulder with curry powder, salt, pepper, and laurel leaves. Boil the shoulder until meat is tender. Air dry for two hours by hanging on a roasting rack. Deep-fry the shoulder until crispy. Set aside.

For the sauce, sauté garlic, onion, and pork. Add vinegar, soy sauce, laurel and seasonings. Simmer until reduced.

2

adobadong bibe
native duck adobo

INGREDIENTS
1 tbsp. butter
2 tbsps. olive oil
700 gms. bibe (native duck),
  chopped into serving pieces
5 tbsps. wine vinegar
10 cloves garlic, slightly crushed
1/2 tbsp. green peppercorns
1/3 cup green olives
1 tbsp. patis
3 tbsps. brandy
1/2 cup chicken stock

procedure
Heat butter and oil in pan. Sweat the duck to render the duck's fat. Let the duck turn brown before adding the garlic. Pressure-cook until tender. Add garlic and cook until slightly brown. Add vinegar and let simmer. Do not stir. Add pepper and olives. Add patis and brandy. Then add the chicken stock and continue simmering until the desired consistency of the sauce is reached.

3

kinunot na pagi
ray in coconut cream

INGREDIENTS

2 cloves garlic, crushed
1 medium onion, coarsely
    chopped
1/2 cup gata (coconut cream)
1/2 kg. pagi (ray)
10 gms. ginger, cut into strips
10 gms. bamboo shoots,
    cut into strips
2 pcs. siling sigang
    (cooking chilies)
1 tbsp. vinegar
salt and pepper to taste

procedure

Boil the pagi about 10 minutes until the black skin can be removed. Drain the water to lessen the strong odor of the fish. Remove the black skin and wad the meat, flake, then set aside.

In a carajay over high heat, boil coconut milk, garlic, onions, and ginger. Stir constantly. When the oil appears, add the pagi flakes and vinegar. When the fish is almost done, add the bamboo shoots and sili. Season with salt and pepper.

sinaing na tambakol sa bawang at kamias
tambakol steak in garlic and kamias

INGREDIENTS
200 gms. pork fat, diced
3 large kamias, quartered
400 gms. tambakol steak,
  seasoned with some
  salt and water
1/2 cup soy sauce
1 tbsp. salt and pepper mix
water
1 tsp. garlic

procedure
Place pork fat on the bottom of the palayok. Add a layer of kamias and garlic. Season fish steak with some salt and wrap in banana leaf (1 pc. wrap). Put fish on top of the fat and kamias layer. Pour some water just enough to cover the fish. Add the soy sauce, salt and pepper. Place over heat. Let it simmer for about 3 hours or until the fish bones are soft enough to eat.

adobong pusit sa saging
squid in banana blossoms

INGREDIENTS
1/8 cup banana blossoms,
    dried, soaked in warm water
700 gms. squid body,
    cleaned and membrane
    taken out, cut into florettes
3 tbsps. vinegar
2 tbsps. oil
8 cloves garlic
2 tbsps. patis
1 tsp. green peppercorns
2 tbsps. Japanese soy sauce
1 medium onion
1 semi-ripe or ripe saba
    (plantain), dredged in
    flour, sliced lengthwise,
    and deep-fried

procedure

Sauté garlic and onion in oil until slightly brown. Add the squid and the rehydrated banana blossoms. Add vinegar and simmer. Don't stir until vinegar boils and releases its acidic odor. Add all other ingredients. Before serving, top with deep-fried saba.

the chef says:

How to clean squid: Pull out innards, head, tentacles and wash out ink in running water. Peel off membrane. Soak in water.

adobong paa ng manok sa gata
chicken feet in coconut cream

INGREDIENTS
1 tbsp. cooking oil
2 cloves garlic
2 ginger
2 onions
1/2 tsp. vinegar
1/2 cup gata (coconut cream)
1/2 cup lemongrass
4 pcs. paa ng manok
  (chicken feet)

procedure
Boil chicken feet. Set aside. Sauté garlic, ginger, and onions in oil. Add chicken feet. Put vinegar, gata and lemongrass. Simmer until chicken feet are tender and have absorbed the coconut cream.

adobong sili
chili adobo

INGREDIENTS
1 tbsp. oil
1 tbsp. garlic
1 tbsp. onion
1 tbsp. sili (chili)
1 tbsp. vinegar
1 tsp. anchovies, diluted
   in water (bagoong
   Balayan)

procedure
Sauté garlic and onions in oil. Add sili and vinegar and bring to a boil. Add anchovies, simmer and serve.

arobong camaru
cricket adobo

INGREDIENTS
50 gms. camaru, deep-fried
1 tbsp. oil
1 clove garlic
onion
ginger
1 tbsp. vinegar
1 1/2 tsps. soy sauce
1 tsp. white sugar

procedure

Deep-fry camaru in oil. Set aside. Sauté garlic, onion and ginger in oil. Add camaru. Put in vinegar. Don't stir until vinegar boils and releases its acidic odor. Add soy sauce and white sugar to taste.

the chef says:

Camaru or mole crickets are a main source of protein and minerals. They are harvested at the onset of the rainy season when they start leaving their burrows in the rice paddies.

binagoongang baboy
pork in bagoong

INGREDIENTS
*400 gms. pork belly, cut
    into 1/2" squares*
2 tbsps. vinegar
1 tsp. white pepper
1 tsp. garlic
pinch of salt or patis
1 tbsp. oil
2/3 cup bagoong alamang
2 medium tomatoes
2 tbsps. chicken stock

procedure
Sweat the pork in oil until pork cooks in its own lard. Sauté garlic in the pork lard. Add vinegar and simmer. Don't stir until vinegar boils and releases its acidic odor. Add pepper. Add a little patis or salt and continue simmering over low heat until pork is brown. Add onion and tomatoes. Continue stir-frying until tomatoes are cooked and limp. Add bagoong and chicken stock.

the chef says:
You can add sugar to this dish like the folks in Central Luzon do. Washing the *bagoong* makes it less salty. In some cases, freshly caught alamang, instead of bagoong, that is lightly salted and fermented is used.

Apalit adobo
Pampango style adobo

INGREDIENTS

400 gms. pork, cut
    into 1" cubes
400 gms. chicken
100 gms. chicken heart
100 gms. beef liver, cut
    into 1/4" cubes
100 gms. pork kidney, cut
    into 1" cubes
100 gms. chicken giblets,
    cleaned
50 gms. chicken blood,
    cut into 1" cubes
1/3 cup vinegar
2 tbsps. oil
1/2 tbsp. cracked pepper
1 tbsp. garlic
3/4 tbsp. salt
4 tbsps. patis
3 tbsps. pork lard
2 cups chicken stock

procedure

Sauté garlic in oil until slightly brown. Add pork cubes, chicken, chicken heart, beef liver, pork kidney, chicken giblets and chicken blood. Add vinegar, pepper then patis. Take out chicken giblets and heart, beef liver and chicken blood. Continue braising. Add all variety meats when chicken and pork are tender and sauce turns brown. Simmer for 15 minutes then separate from meat. Set aside. Fry meat in pork lard until brown and lightly crusty. Serve with sauce on the side.

11

adobong Tsino
Chinese pork adobo

INGREDIENTS

1 kg. pork ribs, cut up with
   soft ribs, cartilage
   included
3 tbsps. vinegar
1/2 tbsp. whole peppercorns
1 tbsp. garlic
1/2 tsp. salt
1/2 tsp. patis
2 tbsps. oil
1 tbsp. sliced ginger
1/2 tsp. five-spice powder
whole sanque or star anise
3 tbsps. soy sauce
3 cups chicken

1 tsp. sugar
1/4 cup anisado or rice wine
   (sioktong)

procedure

In a wok, heat oil and stir-fry garlic and ginger together. Add meat and brown. Add vinegar and simmer. Don't stir until vinegar boils and releases its acidic odor. Add pepper. Add all other ingredients together and simmer until sauce turns light or golden brown.

the chef says:

A variation of this dish requires an addition of radish chunks simmered 20-30 minutes before serving. This Chinese adobo (with pork ribs deboned) can be used as a filling for a Chinese snack called *kuapao*.

adobong tugak quing dilo
frog legs adobo with turmeric

INGREDIENTS
700 gms. frog legs
1/8 cup vinegar
1/4 tsp. cracked pepper
1 tsp. garlic
1 tbsp. patis
2 tbsps. oil
1 tbsp. finely chopped
   fresh turmeric
1/3 cup chicken stock

procedure
Sauté garlic in oil until slightly brown. Add frog legs. Stir-fry until brown. Add vinegar, fresh turmeric then simmer. Don't stir until vinegar boils and releases its acidic odor. Add cracked pepper. Add patis and continue simmering over low heat until frog legs are tender.

the chef says:
You can also use chicken, catfish and peeled shrimp if you can't find frog legs.

chicken adobo
with coco cream

INGREDIENTS
700 gms.chicken
3 tbsps. vinegar
1/4 tsp. cracked pepper
1 tbsp. garlic
1/4 tsp. salt
1/4 cup patis
2 tbsps. oil
1 1/8 pack instant coconut
    cream dissolved in
    1 cup water
4 finger chilies

procedure

Sauté garlic in oil until slightly brown. Add chicken while stir-frying.

Add vinegar and simmer. Don't stir until vinegar boils and releases its acidic odor. Add pepper. Add patis and continue simmering over low heat until chicken is tender. Add coconut cream and finger chilies. Simmer.

the chef says:

To add a deep-toasted coconut flavor to this dish, let the coconut cream simmer until it curdles. Some provinces enhance this dish by adding young alagaw leaves, young mango leaves, bamboo shoots or fresh turmeric.

adobong pang-inuman
drinkers' adobo

INGREDIENTS
1 kg. special meat of the season
3 tbsps. vinegar
1/2 tsp. cracked peppercorns
2 tsps. garlic
1/2 tsp. salt
2 tbsps. patis
2 tbsps. oil
2 pcs. bay leaf
2-3 bird's eye chilies
1/2- 2/3 cup gin
1/4 cup soy sauce
4 cups stock

procedure
Sauté garlic in oil until slightly brown. Add special meat of the season. Brown the meat while stir-frying. Add vinegar. Don't stir until vinegar boils and releases its acidic odor. Add pepper, then patis. Add chili, soy sauce, bay leaf, deep-fried onions and gin. Cover and simmer until meat is tender.

the chef says:
Special meat of the season refers to any domesticated or wild meat.

Batangas beef adobo

INGREDIENTS
1/2 kg. beef short ribs
3 tbsps. vinegar
1/2 tbsp. whole peppercorns
2 tsps. garlic
1/2 tsp. salt
2 tbsps. patis
2 pcs. bay leaf
4 tbsps. achuete oil
1 tbsp. soy sauce
4 cups chicken stock
1/2 sanque (star anise)

procedure
Sauté garlic in achuete oil. Add short ribs then brown. Add vinegar and simmer. Don't stir until vinegar boils and releases its acidic odor. Add pepper. Add patis, soy sauce and bay leaf while simmering. Braise short ribs in 4 cups stock in a covered pot for 2 hours or pressure cook for 30 minutes.

chicken pork adobo

INGREDIENTS
400 gms. pork, cut into
    1" cubes
400 gms. chicken
3 tbsps. vinegar
1/4 tsp. cracked peppercorns
8 cloves garlic, crushed or
    2 small heads of native garlic
1/2 tsp. salt
2 tbsps. patis
2 tbsps. oil
1 cup stock

procedure
Sauté garlic in oil. Press garlic to infuse flavor in the oil. Add pork and chicken, then brown while stir-frying. Sweat the meat until golden brown. Add vinegar and simmer. Don't stir until vinegar boils and releases its acidic odor. Add pepper then patis. Braise meat in 1 cup stock, scraping the sides and bottom of the pan.

the chef says:

For a country-style flavor, add 80 gms. cleaned chicken liver while sautéing the meats. When the meats have changed color, mash the chicken liver into the simmering liquid to incorporate it into the sauce. Add one bay leaf for more flavor.

spicy chicken adobo in green peppercorns and lemongrass

INGREDIENTS
800 gms. chicken
1 tsp. cracked green
  peppercorns
8 stalks lemongrass
  (lower stalks only)
3 tbsps. vinegar
8 cloves garlic
1/2 tsp. salt
2 tbsps. patis
2 tbsps. oil
1 pc. bird's eye chili

procedure

Pound the stalks of lemongrass with the back of a knife. Marinate the chicken with lemongrass overnight. Sauté garlic in oil, add chicken until golden brown. Add vinegar but don't stir. Add peppercorns, salt, patis and chili.

18

bringhe
rice in turmeric topped with adobo and Chinese sausage

INGREDIENTS
400 gms. pork, cut into
  1" cubes
400 gms. chicken
3 tbsps. vinegar
1/4 tsp. cracked peppercorns
8 cloves large garlic, crushed
1/2 tsp. salt
2 tbsps. patis
2 tbsps. oil
1 cup chicken stock

RICE
1 medium red onion, chopped
1 bay leaf
1 stalk lemongrass, crushed
  with cleaver
1/4 kg. malagkit, washed
1/4 kg. milagrosa or
  dinorado rice
1 cup coconut milk, the first
  pure extract, then add
  one cup water to extract
  remaining mix

CHICKEN STOCK
10 gms. dilaw (turmeric),
  crushed
1/4 cup fried and sliced
  Chinese chorizo
1/4 cup raisins

19

procedure

Sauté the chicken and pork with half a teaspoon of garlic and pork fat. Brown everything gently. Add vinegar and patis and braise gently. Season with salt and pepper. In a deep pan or *kawali,* heat oil and sauté half a teaspoon of garlic. Add onion, bay leaf, lemongrass, rice, coconut milk, chicken stock, and turmeric. Continue cooking while folding mixture regularly. Line the bottom of another pan with a banana leaf. Pour in the rice mixture and top with chicken and pork adobo, Chinese sausage and raisins. Cover for 15 minutes.

adobado mushroom

INGREDIENTS

200 gms. fresh button
mushrooms
1 tbsp. butter
2 tbsps. olive oil
2 tbsps. finely chopped
garlic
1 tbsp. finely chopped
celery
1 tsp. liquid seasoning
1/2 tsp. pepper
1/2 tsp. salt
1 bay leaf
1 tbsp. chopped parsley
1 tbsp. wine vinegar
2 tbsps. brandy
1 tbsp. Spanish paprika or
paprika pikante

procedure

Sauté garlic in hot butter and olive oil until golden brown. Add mushrooms, paprika, celery, wine vinegar, salt, pepper, bay leaf, liquid seasoning and chopped parsley. Add or flame with brandy.

adobong pusit sa tinta
black squid adobo

INGREDIENTS
1 kg. pusit (squid)
4 tbsps. vinegar
1/2 tsp. cracked peppercorns
1 tsp. garlic
1 tsp. salt
2 1/2 tbsps. patis
2 tbsps. oil
1/4 cup onion
1 1/2 tsps. squid ink

procedure

Sauté garlic until light brown. Add pusit and stir-fry. Add all the squid ink. Add vinegar. Simmer, but don't stir. Add pepper, patis and continue simmering over low heat.

the chef says:

To prepare squid, pull out tentacles from body, take out cartilage and squeeze out squid ink from torso and eyes into a cup.

pininyahang adobo
adobo with pineapple

INGREDIENTS
700 gms. pork, cubed pork
  or pork liver
3 tbsps. vinegar
1/4 cup pineapple chunks
1/2 tsp. cracked peppercorns
8 cloves garlic, crushed
1/4 tsp. salt
2 tbsps. patis
2 tbsps. oil

procedure
Sauté garlic in oil until light brown. Add pork then brown, while stir-frying. Add vinegar and simmer. Don't stir until vinegar boils and releases its acidic odor. Add pepper, patis and continue simmering until pork is tender. Throw in pineapple chunks, simmer a while then serve.

adobong kangkong
swamp cabbage adobo

INGREDIENTS
2 bundles kangkong
   (swamp cabbage)
2 tbsps. vinegar
1/8 tsp. pepper
1 tsp. finely chopped garlic
a dash of salt
1/2 tbsp. patis
2 tbsps. oil
5 tbsps. soy sauce
1/4 cup chopped onions

procedure
Sauté garlic in oil until golden brown. Add onion. Turn to high heat and add kangkong. Spritz with vinegar while stir-frying. Add all other ingredients.

the chef says:

Instead of kangkong, you can also use *sitaw* (yard beans) cut into 2 1/2 inch pieces or *segadillas* (winged beans) cut into 1 cm. stars.

sisig lechon
roasted pig sisig

INGREDIENTS
200 gms. chopped lechon
  (roasted pig head)
50 gms. chopped roasted
  pork liver
1 tsp. garlic
1/3 cup finely chopped onions
3 tbsps. vinegar
1 tbsp. Worcestershire sauce
1/2 tsp. liquid seasoning
1 1/2 tsp. salt
1/2 tbsp. cracked peppercorns
1/2 tsp. soy sauce
1/2 tsp. chili powder
1 1/2 tsps. oil

procedure

Simmer onions and vinegar together until vinegar is reduced and onions are cooked. Set aside. Mix together chopped pig head, pork liver, Worcestershire sauce, soy sauce, salt, pepper and chili powder. In a pan, sauté garlic with oil, add vinegar-infused onions and mix with lechon. Simmer mixture until liquid is reduced. Serve on a sizzling platter.

kilawin/adobong labanos
radish adobo with offal

INGREDIENTS

1/2 cup/100 gms. sliced pork meat
1/2 cup/100 gms. pork liver, cut into strips
1/2 cup/100 gms. heart
1/2 cup/100 gms. pork spleen (optional)
50 gms. kidney
1 pc. tomato, chopped
1/4 cup chopped onion
1 1/2 tbsps. cracked white peppercorns
1 1/2 tbsps. garlic
2 tbsps. patis
1 1/2 tbsps. oil
turmeric
radish (labanos)

to prepare pork kidney

Take out all the fat and membranes, leaving the smooth part of the kidney. Wash in running water. Rub on salt then cut into strips. Soak in water for an hour, changing the water after every 15 minutes. Wash kidneys with vinegar.

procedure

Sauté garlic until slightly brown, then add onion. Add pork, liver, heart, kidney, and turmeric. Add tomatoes, patis and labanos. Add vinegar, do not stir. Put in labanos, pepper, and salt. Serve when radish slices are cooked but still firm.

lagat na kanduli sa dilaw
braised catfish in turmeric

INGREDIENTS
1.2 kg. kanduli (white catfish)
1/4 tsp. cracked white
    peppercorns
1 tsp. garlic
3 tbsps. vinegar
1 tbsp. patis
2 tbsps. oil
1 tbsp. finely chopped turmeric
1/2 cup thick coconut cream
6 pcs. alagaw leaves
1 tbsp. onion
2 pcs. finger chilies

procedure
Sauté garlic in oil until slightly brown. Add onion. Add kanduli, then brown while stir-frying. Add turmeric. Add vinegar and simmer. Don't stir until vinegar boils and then add alagaw leaves. Add pepper, patis and coconut cream. Simmer.

the chef says:
One can use native catfish or fresh saltwater eel for this recipe. I've also used other fish such as cod and salmon quite successfully.

sisig pusong saging
banana heart sisig

INGREDIENTS
2 pcs. banana heart
1 tbsp. finely chopped garlic
1/8 tsp. pepper
3 tbsps. vinegar
2 1/2 tbsps. patis
1/2 tsp. salt
2 tbsps. oil
1/4 cup chopped onions

procedure
Peel banana heart until you reach the white part. Slice this thinly against the grain into rings. Mash with salt and squeeze out the juices to take away the tannic sap. Do this three times. Sauté in oil, garlic, and add vinegar and pepper. Simmer, then add patis. Bring to high heat and stir-fry or toss in wok until there is no more excess. Serve hot.

the chef says:
You can add shrimps and pork or a cup of thick coconut cream while stir-frying.

This dish was widely eaten during wars and famines when people wanted meat-like textures in their food.

adobo de campesino

INGREDIENTS
700 gms. pork cut into
   1/2" cubes
1 cup sitaw (yard beans)
3 tbsps. vinegar
1/4 tsp. pepper
8 cloves garlic
1/2 tsp. salt
2 tbsps. patis
3 tbsps. achuete oil

to make achuete oil
1 cup achuete seeds
1 cup cooking oil

Heat oil in pan and add achuete seeds. Simmer for a few minutes until oil is reddish-orange in color.

procedure

Sauté garlic in achuete oil until slightly brown. Add pork and stir-fry until brown. Add vinegar and simmer. Don't stir until vinegar boils and releases its acidic odor. Add pepper and patis and continue simmering over low heat until pork is tender. Before serving, ladle out the pork into a serving dish. Toss yard beans in the pan. Serve together in a platter.

the chef says:
This is a favorite Southern Luzon recipe that must have originated from the Spanish friars. The use of achuete or annatto oil is also used in other Hispanized colonies.

bopis

INGREDIENTS
3 tbsps. achuete oil
1 tbsp. minced garlic
3/4 cup chopped onions
1/4 cup chopped tomatoes
100 gms. pork lungs,
   cleaned and diced
100 gms. pork heart,
   cleaned and diced
100 gms. pork liver,
   cleaned and diced
1 tbsp. soy sauce
1/2 cup vinegar
4 cup water
1/4 tbsps. sliced radish
2 tbsps. chopped green
   bell pepper
1/2 tsp. freshly cracked
   black peppercorns
salt to taste

procedure

Sauté garlic, onions and tomatoes in oil. Add lungs, heart and liver and stir-fry for a few minutes. Pour in soy sauce, vinegar and water. Let it boil (DO NOT STIR) and simmer over low heat for 30 minutes. Blend in remaining ingredients and continue simmering until most of the liquid has evaporated or until the heart and lungs are tender. Serve hot. Makes 4 servings.

adobo flakes

INGREDIENTS
*800 gms. mixed pork belly
    cubes or chicken meat*
3 tbsps. vinegar
1/4 tsp. cracked peppercorns
8 cloves garlic
1/2 tsp. salt
2 tbsps. soy sauce
2 tbsps. patis
2 tbsps. oil

procedure

Sauté garlic in oil until slightly brown. Stir-fry pork until brown. Add vinegar and simmer.

Don't stir until vinegar boils and releases its acidic odor. Add pepper, soy sauce, patis and continue simmering over low heat until meat is brown and tender. Flake the very tender meat with your ladle and debone meat parts. Continue simmering until liquid is reduced into the oil. This will fry your adobo until you have brown colored flakes.

the chef says:

This dish is excellent as breakfast and snack fare and can be transformed as bar chow especially by adding chilies or more spices.

adobo mates

An excellent side dish for seafood
and fish adobo:

Grill three eggplants. Peel off skin while still hot.
Roughly chop eggplants. Add 2 tbsps. onions, 1 tbsp.
calamansi juice, 2 tbsps. extra thick coconut milk, 1/2
tsp. salt and a pinch of black pepper.

manibalang mango salad

Slice 2 almost ripened but slightly tart mangoes.
Add 1/4 cup onion, 1/4 chopped tomatoes and 2 tbsps.
bagoong guisado.

bamboo shoots and water chestnut salad

1/4 cup canned bamboo shoots, julienned
1 cup sliced water chestnuts

Toss together with 1 tbsp. hoisin sauce, 1 tsp. soy sauce, 1 tsp. sugar, and 1 tsp. rice wine.

glossary

achuete/ atsuete
also called achiote or annatto. Can be bought powdered or in oil form at Filipino supermarkets. Oil can be extracted by lightly simmering seeds in warm cooking oil for 15-30 minutes.

bagoong
is shrimp paste made by salting very small shrimps and pressing them into vats. This is used as a condiment.

carajay
a deep, round-bottomed frying pan

chilies *(Capsicum annum/Capsicum frutescens)*
though there are several varieties of chilies, most widely used in Philippine cuisine are the green finger chilies and *labuyo* or the wild bird's eye chilies. It is locally known as *sili.*

coconut or coco cream
extracted from pressed grated mature coconuts. The first pressing or thickest pressing is called *kakang gata* which gives a sweetish, creamy texture to adobo dishes.

five-spice powder *(ngo-hiong)*

a mixture used widely in China and Vietnam and is used to roast meat and poultry and to flavor marinades. The most common five-spice mix consists of cinnamon or cassia together with fennel seeds, cloves, fagara and star anise.

kamias

an acidic but edible fruit used for local stews (sinigang).

lechon

roasted pig

lemongrass *(Cymbopogon citratus)*

known in the Philippines as *tanglad*, has the aroma and taste that is distinctly lemon-like because it contains citral which is also present in lemon peel. It is used in the production of artificial lemon flavor.

palayok

a clay pot with cover

patis *(nuoc-mam)*

a clear, brown liquid extracted from heavily salted fish pressed in sealed vats. Patis nuances and strengths may vary from cheesy to a highly fermented odor. This can be extracted from shrimps, small or big fish depending on the province it comes from.

pepper *(Piper nigrum)*

clustered berries growing from a vine, normally green when fresh and black when dried and shrivelled.

Black pepper has a warm woody smell that is fresh, pungent and is agreeably aromatic while green pepper is sharp and more herbal in character. White pepper, which is hotter, is dried peppercorns without the dark skin.

saba
plantain or cooking banana

star anise *(Illiciuym verum)*
pungently licorice-like and has a distinct note. Star anise in the Philippines, commonly called *sanque*, is used reverently for food with Chinese or mestizo influences.

tambakol
yellowfin tuna

turmeric *(Curcuma langa)*
In the Philippines, turmeric is used mainly to neutralize fish odors in seafood and the raw odor of chicken. Turmeric is locally called *dilaw.*

vinegar
Locally called *suka*, it varies from province to province depending on the agricultural produce. Most popular are made from coconut water, coconut sap, sugar, pineapple and other palm saps. These types of vinegar determine regional characteristics present in adobo recipes of different provinces.